# ASHBOU~~~
# & DOVEDALE

BRITAIN IN OLD PHOTOGRAPHS

# ASHBOURNE
# & DOVEDALE

MARY WINSTONE

SUTTON PUBLISHING LIMITED

Sutton Publishing Limited
Phoenix Mill · Thrupp · Stroud
Gloucestershire · GL5 2BU

First published 1996

**British Library Cataloguing in Publication Data**
A catalogue record for this book is available from the
British Library.

ISBN 0-7509-0900-5

Typeset in 10/12 Perpetua.
Typesetting and origination by
Sutton Publishing Limited.
Printed in Great Britain by
Ebenezer Baylis, Worcester.

# CONTENTS

# INTRODUCTION

The earliest records name Ashbourne as 'Esseburne' – a name that is derived from 'ash' tree and 'burne', or stream – presumably after Henmore Brook, a tributary of the River Dove that runs through the town. In 1086 Domesday Book records a church and a priest here, with the manor being held by William the Conqueror. It passed from royal hands to William Ferrers in 1186, and sixty-seven years later to the Cokayne family. The Cokaynes had been in the region since the twelfth century, at first acquiring a dubious reputation as gang leaders who were involved in local warfare between rival families and factions. By the sixteenth century, however, they were eminently respectable: Sir Thomas Cokayne (1479–1537) was knighted by Henry VIII at the Siege of Tournai and accompanied the king on the Field of the Cloth of Gold, while his grandson, another Thomas (1520–92), was also knighted and served as high sheriff of Derbyshire four times.

In 1671 Sir Aston Cokayne sold Ashbourne Hall and the estate to the Boothbys. Subsequent owners included Thomas Hayston Frank, who turned the Hall into a hotel, and Joseph Harrison, under whom the estate was broken up. Today part of the Hall, much altered, is the town's public library.

Ashbourne itself was described by the nineteenth-century novelist George Eliot as a 'pretty town within sight of the blue hills'. Today it is still attractive, with its primarily stone and brick buildings (although some have earlier timber framing hidden underneath) dominated by the thirteenth-century spire of St Oswald's Church. In 1257 the town was granted a charter to allow stalls on the large triangular market-place, which stretches from the George and Dragon down to St John Street and the Butchery. The later partial infilling occurred when some of these stalls became permanent. Ashbourne gradually became a thriving market centre for the surrounding area, becoming a royal borough in 1276. There were fairs selling cattle and sheep, cheese fairs four times a year and horse fairs three times a year. There was even a hiring fair, where servants were bought and sold: this was known as Gawboys or Gayboys Fair. Today there are still markets every Thursday and Saturday, and a cattle market on Thursdays.

Much of the town dates from the sixteenth to nineteenth centuries, with some very fine buildings on Church Street and St John Street. The Old Grammar School (founded by Queen Elizabeth in 1585) stands opposite The Mansion – where Dr Samuel Johnson often visited Dr John Taylor – on Church Street, while the mid-Georgian Green Man and Black's Head Royal Hotel has an unusual signboard slung across the street as well as a picturesque courtyard. The town hall, which overlooks the market-place, was built in 1861 to a design by Benjamin Wilson of Derby. Many of Ashbourne's wealthier inhabitants gave donations towards this, as in the past they had generously endowed an unusually large number of almshouses in the town: Spalden Almshouses (1723–4, to the south-east of the church), Owfield's Almshouses (1614–30, Church Street), Pegg's Almshouses (1669, adjacent to Owfield's), Clergymen's Widows' Almshouses (1753, Church Street) and Coopers' Almshouses (1800, Derby Road).

Expansion of the town in the 1920s saw the construction of Cokayne Avenue, Spalden Avenue and Boothby Avenue. A First World War memorial was erected and the recreation ground was laid out. The Park Estate, near the fishpond, was to follow; this took in the Congregational Church cricket pitch.

Ashbourne is often known as the Gateway to the Peak, because it stands on the edge of the Peak District National Park, an area of great beauty. For this reason Dovedale (arguably the most picturesque and the most famous of all the dales, as well as the closest to Ashbourne) is included in this book.

It is hoped that *Ashbourne & Dovedale* will bring back many happy memories for all who know the area well, and will encourage anyone who is unfamiliar with this beautiful part of Derbyshire to explore it in more detail.

Sir Aston Cokayne, from a print published 1 November 1796. He was the last of the Cokaynes to live in Ashbourne. Born in Mappleton, Sir Aston was the great grandson of Sir Thomas. Sir Aston was forced to sell his estates in 1671; his Ashbourne estate was bought by the Boothbys.

# THE CHURCH

*The church from the east and the graveyard, 1842. The chancel
and the 212 ft high spire are shown to good effect.*

St Oswald's Church from the Sudbury Road, 1842. According to a brass memorial on the south wall of the south transept, the church was dedicated in 1241 in honour of St Oswald, King of Northumberland and martyr, by the Venerable Father the Lord Hugh Patishul, Bishop of Coventry. It is thought that the chancel dates from this time, having survived the town fire, which took place according to Pegge in 1252. The first vicarage was built on Keepers Meadow, and was a gift from the Dean of Lincoln, previously vicar of this parish. Three more vicarages were built, in 1290, 1722 and 1856.

A christening in the south transept at St Oswald's, 1842. The thirteenth-century font is still in the church. Note the carving on the pews, and the galleries: these dated from 1760 and were taken down in the 1880s.

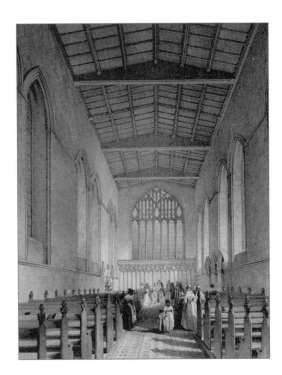

The wedding of Letitia Percival to Major Powlett of Ashbourne Hall, 1842. This is the chancel, looking towards the high altar at the east end. The seven-light east window dates from the end of the fourteenth century.

The Boothby Chapel is notable for its monuments to the Cokayne and Boothby families. Note the funeral hatchment to the top right of this engraving.

The nave and pulpit, 1849. Nave and chancel together are 176 ft long.

The north transept and the Boothby Chapel.

Restoration of the tower and spire, 1891. Much restoration and repair work had been done in 1837–40 by L.N. Cottingham, while the chancel was restored (and given its battlements) by Sir George Gilbert Scott in 1876–8.

Church Avenue. These trees were given to the church by parishioners and business people.

Penelope Boothby (1785–91), painted by Sir Joshua Reynolds. Penelope was the only daughter of Sir Brooke and Lady Susannah Boothby, and it is said that her stricken parents parted at her grave.

Penelope's memorial in the Boothby Chapel is the work of Thomas Banks, and is constructed of white marble. When Queen Charlotte saw the statue of Penelope lying asleep – it was exhibited at the Royal Academy exhibition – she burst into tears, or so the story goes. There are inscriptions in Italian, French, Latin and English, the last of which reads: 'She was in form and intellect most exquisite. The unfortunate parents ventured their all on this frail Bark. And the wreck was total.'

Canon Morris, the vicar, stands outside the west door holding the cockerel weather vane, 1890s. He is accompanied by Mr Turnbull and Mr Thomas Edge, churchwardens. A window in the south aisle commemorates Monica and Dorothea Turnbull, Mr Turnbull's daughters, who died in a fire at the family home, Sandybrook Hall, in 1904.

Sunday School children and teachers on Church Banks, across the road from the church, 1890s.

The opening of the new Queen Elizabeth's Grammar School, 1909. After a service at St Oswald's the congregation paraded up to the new school on Green Road; it was officially opened by the Duke of Devonshire. In the background of this picture it is just possible to make out the churchyard gates. The stone gatepiers are interesting: each obelisk rests on four stone skulls.

Distinctive in their blue veils, these members of the Sunday School are attending a children's festival, 1930. The picture includes the following: Vera Colbourne, Betty Frost, Nancy Hill, Marion Knight, Sybil Richardson, Kathleen Hancock, Margaret Kirkland, Jean Shuttleworth, Joan Hill, Barbara Rowe, Joyce Mottram, June Hollinshead, Margaret Hancock, Irene Purdy, Kathleen Cundy, Nora Grindey, Joan Mottram, Dorothy Rowe, Jessie Potter, Pauline Cundy, Laura Grindey, Madge Allen, Hilda Blake, Margaret Cundy, Doreen Slater, Pam Slater, Audrey Tomlinson and Helen Gallimore.

# AROUND THE TOWN

*The corner of St John Street. A newsagent and tobacconist is on the left, while Cash's shoe shop, later to move to the market-place, is on the right.*

The Old Grammar School, founded by royal charter in 1585. The seal depicts Queen Elizabeth I seated in majesty with the five founding fathers of the school. They were Sir Thomas Cokayne of Ashbourne Hall, William Bradbourne of Lea Hall, Tissington, Thomas Carter of the Middle Temple, London, Thomas Hurt of Ashbourne Green and William Jackson of Ashbourne. The building was finally finished in 1603, at a total cost of about £400. Dr Samuel Johnson applied for a job as undermaster, but was turned down.

Next door to the Old Grammar School is the Grey House, dating from the mid-eighteenth century. Its large porch and first-floor Venetian window are similar to that of The Mansion.

The Mansion is opposite the Old Grammar School. It was built in 1680 by Benjamin Taylor, but the brick façade dates from the mid-eighteenth century: it was added by Dr John Taylor, Benjamin's grandson, to the designs of James Pickford, the well-known Derby architect. Pickford also designed the octagonal, and domed, drawing room and the imposing entrance hall. The extensive gardens, which included a lake, stretched almost as far as The Paddock, just behind Lloyds Bank.

Just beyond The Mansion is The Old House. This was at one time a dower house, for unmarried daughters and widows, and was owned by the Hayne family. Later it was owned by Dr Hollick, whose family lived here; he shared his surgery with Dr Sadler.

The Wheatsheaf Hotel, when Edwin Wragg was proprietor. This photograph predates 1884, when the Crompton Evans Union Bank took over the premises. The bank remained in the market-place while alterations were carried out. Some of the stone was taken away and used in the building of houses on Clifton Road, which now belong to Nestlés. Mr Wither was manager of the Crompton Evans Union Bank from 1885 until his retirement in 1921; Mr Coulson, chief cashier, took his place.

J. Osborne, printer, bookseller and stationer, St John Street. Osborne's was also a chemist, and had another shop just up the road where Cook's is now. The dispensers worked in a shop just across the road, making primrose ointment and various cough mixtures. On the left of this photograph can be seen the signboard for the Green Man and Black's Head Royal Hotel, which was once a gibbet.

The Green Man and Black's Head Royal Hotel. The gallows signboard across the road depicts both halves of the name: the green man appears on a conventional board, while the black's head is carved from wood – smiling in one direction, miserable on the other. The two inns were separate until 1826, when Mr Wood of the Green Man bought the Black's Head from Sir Brooke Boothby, who was losing money through gambling. The 'Royal' was added after a brief visit by Princess Victoria in 1832. The Black's Head had acted as Ashbourne's assembly rooms from 1770 to 1825, while the installation of the new organ at St Oswald's in 1710 had been celebrated in the Black's Head's great parlour with a concert of instrumental and vocal music. The cockpit was once in the Black's Head's yard.

Mrs Wallis tending her plants in the Green Man's yard, 1930s. The steps to Boswell Bar are still there today. At Christmas the hotel's entrance was full of turkeys, game and hams hanging from the ceiling.

Millbank House, 34 St John Street, the home of Mr T.J. Potter, corn merchant. In the seventeenth century this had been the Star and Garter inn, and still had large cellars with thrawls (stone supports for barrels of beer); the building has now been converted into flats. To the right is the shop window, while at the back was a warehouse for storing corn. This is now a fishing tackle business, and an optician is in the old dining room. The bath house can still be seen at the back.

Thomas John Potter (d. 1924), the author's grandfather, was born in Derby, but moved with his wife and their children, Rhoda and James, to 34 St John Street, Ashbourne. He was a corn merchant, local councillor and amateur photographer: many of the photographs in this book were taken by him – and were rescued from a bonfire in 1940 before too much damage was done.

The garden, Millbank House. It stretches down to the Henmore Brook, and overlooks Shaw Croft.

Mr H.T. Spencer's café in St John Street was originally half the size, but he bought the small shoe shop next door to expand his business. There were several cottages down his yard, a large café that opened on market days, and also a bake house and two garages: the latter are now run by Robin Pearson. It is interesting to note the fake half timbering on this building: the genuine timber frame is underneath! H.T. Spencer and his grandson, Kenneth Pearson, are on this photograph, which dates from 1939.

Lister's High Class Drapery, Carpets and Materials is on the left of this photograph. The Lister family originally came from Lincolnshire. The lamp in front of the shop replaced a market cross, and was in turn removed to make way for traffic turning into Upper St John Street.

Bradley's, coffee merchant and tobacco dealer — a large and busy shop, seen here in the 1890s. It was sandwiched between two drapers: J.W. Blore on the right and W. Abraham on the left. The Bradleys were a well-to-do family, who helped to build the town hall.

Looking down St John Street, decorated with flags, bunting and lanterns. The event is unfortunately not known.

*The building in the centre was demolished as unsafe. The site is occupied by the old People's Rest Hut*

Abraham's Drapery is in the centre of this 1890s photograph, with Bradley's and Blore's to the right. The Green Man and Black's Head sign can just be seen in the distance on the left. Mr and Mrs Abraham lived over the shop. They also had two large semi-detached houses in Windmill Lane, and built two bungalows for retired people on Cokayne Avenue. Mr Cole, greengrocer, took over the shop seen here.

Skellern and Twell's stationer's is on the left, next to Poole's 'hair cutter'. Note the striped barber's pole and, a bit further along, the mounting block. Howell and Marsden's grocer's shop is beyond.

In the 1890s Joseph J. Parker had a small boot and shoe shop in Upper St John Street.

A carriage with nine horses passing along St John Street. Lister's is on the left. The occasion is unknown, but the size of the carriage indicates, perhaps, a carnival procession.

The Memorial Gardens were laid out in memory of the men of Ashbourne who died during the First World War. They contain a bandstand and also a monument of Catherine Booth, wife of William, founder of the Salvation Army. She was born in Sturston Road in 1829.

Ashbourne Hall, once the residence of the Cokayne family and later the Boothbys. Later flats and now the library, this house once also housed a corn merchant's office. In its more illustrious heyday, famous visitors included George Canning, who became prime minister in 1827, and Erasmus Darwin, poet, physician and grandfather of Charles Darwin – who founded a girls' school at the end of St John's Street. This was run by his two illegitimate daughters, the Misses Parker, in a house that had once been a pub called the Upper Nag's Head. It is now the Madge House Nursing Home, named after Dr Madge who lived and worked in the surgery there, which he shared with Dr Eccles.

The fish pond in the grounds of the Hall. In the background can be seen the houses in St John's Street, and also St John the Baptist's Church on Buxton Road. This was built in 1871.

Mrs Blore's drapery business is in the background. Her sister had a millinery business in the old Red Lion Inn. They were both helpful and generous members of St John's Church. This photograph was possibly taken during a carnival procession, after Bradley's moved out.

Callow's Outfitters, still in business today, is on the right of this view of St John Street. Opposite is Hilton's, the poulterer.

The Meynell Hunt in the market-place outside the George and Dragon Hotel for the Boxing Day Meet, 1950s. In the background can be seen two advertisements: 'Players Please' and 'Jaguar Sales and Service: Sanderson and Holmes'.

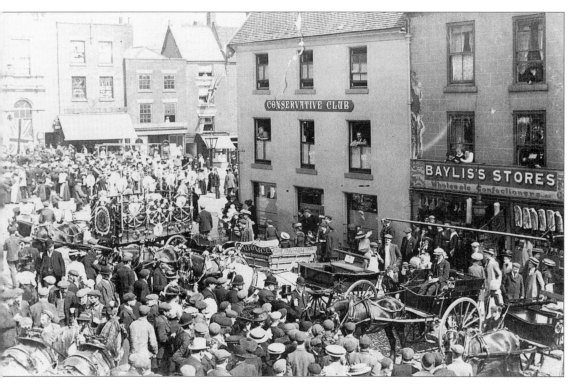

Baylis's Stores and the Conservative Club, during King Edward VII's coronation celebrations, 1901. According to the signboard, Baylis's was a grocer, provisions merchant, wholesale confectioner and importer of foreign goods.

The fire brigade in the market-place, at the end of Buxton Road.

Tiger Yard is one of several yards branching off Victoria Square (usually known as the Butchery), which was part of the original market-place. These yards were created to allow the development of the area behind the frontages of the medieval burgage plots. The Tiger Inn, on the left, is now a restaurant. The building is one of the oldest left in Ashbourne. The Horns, a medieval pub, is opposite, while the building with the stable door may have been the premises of Mr Hart, a photographer. The first Ashbourne gingerbread was made further along the Butchery: the oven still existed in the 1970s. The gingerbread was made by the Porters, whose two sons were confectioners: one went to France to learn the trade, while the other trained with Buzzard's in London. It was not of a biscuity consistency as it is today, but moist with treacle and candied peel.

The Town Hall, built by public subscription in 1861, overlooks the market-place. The large porch with balcony above and the curved pediment can be seen. The Wright Memorial is in the foreground: this was erected in 1874 in memory of Francis Wright, a wealthy and influential local industrialist.

Bamford and Henstock's Printing Office, also bookseller and stationer, with a marching band in the foreground. Their printing press was down Salt Alley Yard. The Red Lion (later Bloor's shop) is on the left.

A horse-drawn carriage travelling up St John Street, with J.C. Lee's, the jeweller, in the background. This shop replaced Lister's, although Lister's retained their drapery business in St John Street.

The White Horse Inn is on the left. It has now been replaced with several houses.

Market Day horse sale in the market-place, 1890s.

Horses and wagons: perhaps this was the same occasion.

The ostlers are looking after the horses and guarding the carts and traps. Water was drawn from the pump by Richard Lynch, licensee of the Ostrich Inn in Union Street.

A fish stall in the market-place.

A horse sale. Kennedy's and Charles Gregory's, flour and corn merchant, are in the background on the left.

From the market-place to St John Street, 1930.

A traction engine passes through the market-place, en route to Ilam Hall from Hereford. The engine was owned by E.H. Davies, removal contractor.

Davenport's, Dig Street. According to the lettering on the door, he was a jeweller, silversmith, watchmaker . . . and optician! The workshop was at the rear.

A flood in Dig Street. Now that the Henmore Brook has been culverted underground there is no longer a problem here.

Compton Bridge, 1903. The Henmore Brook can be seen here flowing under the bridge, before it was culverted.

J. Pitt Woodyatt's cycle business, Compton Bridge. Part of the shoe shop next door is just visible on the right. The sign on the wall proclaims 'Famus [sic] Pitt Cycles, Bassinettes, Mail Carts'. Mr Woodyatt later went to live at the Grey House. His premises at Compton Bridge had housed some of Bonnie Prince Charlie's army, when they passed through the town on their way to Derby.

The Roebuck Inn, at the top of Compton, was owned by Mr and Mrs Haywood. It has now been replaced by houses.

The Wesleyan chapel, Compton, was built in 1822, and was in use until 1880. Later it became Birch's joiner's shop, but has now been demolished. It was replaced by a more prepossessing building in Church Street.

A horse sale or show on Shaw Croft.

Haymaking on Shaw Croft.

A fair on Shaw Croft. The little girl in the centre looks quite pleased with her donkey ride.

Haymaking is thirsty work. The farm worker is being waited on by Mr J. Burns and his grandson, James Potter.

Samuel Jackson with James B. Potter's horse and cart. Jackson lived at the stables in Sandy Lane, and looked after the horses, pigs, wagons and carts.

Rhoda Potter (born 1854), daughter of T.J. Potter, at the stables in Park Lane.

I played here a lot as a boy. We used to dam the little stream at the side of the road

Sandy Lane, now Park Road. The public bath house used to be on the left; it is now Bath House, a private dwelling.

Bellevue Road. The Vicarage and St Oswald's Hospital are further along. Note the posters on the wall at the far left of the photograph.

The Victoria Memorial Hospital, Buxton Road, was opened in 1903 by Queen Victoria's granddaughter, Princess Victoria of Schleswig-Holstein. It was a great asset to the town, and was well equipped with an operating theatre and X-ray equipment – and a mortuary at the rear. Dr Madge and Dr Eccles both worked here during the 1940s, as did many other well-remembered local doctors. The hospital closed in 1964.

Green Road. The Ashbourne Hall estate wall is on the right.

Mixed hockey on The Paddock, early this century. The players include Gladys Porter.

K.D. Bayliss was one of the earliest bus companies in the area, and this was one of their first buses, possibly built on a Model T Ford chassis. It seated fourteen passengers.

One of Bayliss's later buses, an Albion, much larger than the old fourteen seater.

George Harrison's charabanc, seen here outside the Green Man Inn. It must have been uncomfortable for the twelve passengers, with solid tyres and a fairly ineffective hood. Note the Cyclists Touring Club roundel, and the advertisement for Worthington's bottled beer.

Very little is known about this photograph. Mr Wibberly stands in the snow next to the bus, which – although running from Ashbourne to Derby – seems to have been hired from Commercial Car Hirers, Bridge Circus, London.

Edwin Webster's bus outside the Green Man Garage. Webster's of Hognaston was the first company to transport passengers by motor bus to Ashbourne. Sam Rankin, the driver, is leaning on the mudguard. The Green Man Garage advertises that it is an agent for Belsize Cars and also for the Maxwell 30 cwt lorry, which cost a princely £275. Maxwell was an American make, while Belsize were made in Manchester. This photograph probably dates from before 1925, the year in which Belsize closed.

The fire engine on call from the fire station in Hall Lane. It is being followed by Roger Winstone on his bicycle. The station later moved to Cokayne Avenue, to property owned by Ashbourne Hall.

Mr Purdy with his penny farthing. His family were butchers in Compton.

Mr Hilton and friends are standing outside J. Burton's shop, next to the Green Man gallows sign.

The Railway Hotel. Perhaps it is Hannah Mann, the licensee, standing in the doorway.

The Railway Hotel, an interior shot. Is it Hannah Mann on the left?

# ENTERTAINMENT
# & EVENTS

*Ashbourne's territorials marching up Buxton Road to Matlock, August 1914. They were on their way to volunteer to fight in the First World War. On their way they were joined by friends and relatives.*

Ashbourne Town Band at Calwich Abbey near Mayfield, the home of Lady Florence Duncombe. Mr Barton is the bandmaster. The bass drum is still with the band.

Ye Ancient Cricketers, July 1893. This festive group dressed up to celebrate the marriage of HRH the Duke of York to HRH Princess Mary of Teck. Two comic cricket matches were arranged, at the Peveril Hotel and later at Shaw Croft.

The carnival to celebrate the coronation of King George and Queen Mary, 1911. A 'suffragette' is on the right, complete with umbrella and 'Votes for Women' shirt. Other characters include a Red Indian chief, a pierrot and 'Dr Killum', on the left at the front, next to 'St David's Ambulance'.

The coronation carnival procession outside the Station Hotel, Station Road.

The coronation carnival. Mrs Grindey, Miss Porter, Miss Probert and Miss Pegge are on the float.

The coronation carnival procession making its way down Station Road.

The coronation carnival. The elephant seems to be creating a certain amount of amusement.

The Band of Hope. Lady Florence Duncombe did much work for this group of about sixty young ladies, organising lectures, outings and fancy dress parties. Meetings were held on alternate Wednesdays in the National School at 5.45 p.m., with admission costing ½d.

'Ye Ancient Cricketers', Peveril Hotel, Thorpe.

The comic cricket team outside the British Legion in the market-place.

Laying the foundation stone for the new grammar school, 1909.

A group photographed at the opening of Electricity House, School Lane, 11 November 1931. It includes Mrs Birch, Mrs Bond, Mr J. Gadsby, Mrs Madge, Miss Oldham, Mr M. Sadler, Mr J. Sadler, Mrs Stafford and Mr and Mrs Thompson.

The tea party on Buxton Road to celebrate the coronation of Edward VII, 1901.

A house in Buxton Road decorated for Queen
Victoria's jubilee, 1897.

King Edward VII's coronation celebrations in the market-place. Slater's is decorated in the centre.

A church outing to Sandybrook Hall, which belonged to the Turnbulls.

The Shrovetide procession outside the Coach & Horses, Dig Street, when William T. Fowell was the proprietor, 1916. Every Shrove Tuesday and Ash Wednesday Ashbourne witnesses two extraordinary games of football, each lasting up to eight hours, from 2 p.m. to 10 p.m. They are played between the Up'ards (those people who live to the north of Henmore Brook) and the Down'ards (those who live to the south). The pitch is 3 miles long, and the game is played with a white painted football between an unlimited number of players. This riotous event originated, it is thought, in the Middle Ages.

This postcard commemorates the visit of the Prince of Wales to Ashbourne on 21 February 1928, when he started the football game.

The Shrovetiders, 1892. They were photographed in the Green Man yard. Mr Wallis, publican at the Green Man, was to 'turn up' the ball (i.e. start the match) that year. Standing, left to right: J. Cundy, William Coxon, W. Wheeldon, C. Purdy, Alfred Hall, Robert Wallis, J. Cheetham, P. Wallis, J. Frost, J. Coxon, Horace Wells, W. Phillips, W. Drew, Arthur Bladon. Seated: J. Avery, J.W. Blore, F. Tomlinson, J. Wallis, Tom Webster, R. Brown.

J. Harrison is seen holding the ball before the match, 1917. His brother goaled the ball that year. If the first ball is goaled by 5 p.m. another ball is turned up, and play continues.

The Prince of Wales 'turned up' the ball from Lister's garden, 38 St John's Street. A special bridge was erected for the Prince and committee. After this visit Lister's gate was known as the Prince's gate.

I'm doubtful about this caption. I've always supposed that the Derbyshire Yeomanry (cavalry) was completely separate from the Notts & Derby. Regt (Sherwood Foresters — infantry)

The 2nd V.B. Notts and Derbys Regiment, also called the Derbyshire Yeomanry, G Company baggage cart.

Derbyshire Yeomanry G Company volunteers, pictured at Ashbourne while on exercise.

A rifle salute in the market-place by the Yeomanry and others. Unfortunately the occasion has not been recorded.

'Relieving the Garrison': the Derbyshire Yeomanry at camp in Scarborough, 1890s. According to the handwritten additions, Pte. J. Potter's tent is in the foreground, while the guard tent and Cpl. N. Jones are in the background.

# BUILDING THE RAILWAY

*Workmen on the line. The foreman, wearing a bowler hat, is in the foreground.*

The North Staffordshire Railway was opened on 31 May 1858, and Ashbourne became a railway terminus. The line was later extended to Buxton by the London & North Western Railway Company. The first sod was cut by Mr Witham, an old Ashbournian. Sir Thomas Brassey was the line's contractor and engineer; the cost of constructing this 13½ mile long line was £1.5m. The work involved the building of a tunnel 384 yards long from Church Street to the Mappleton Road. These houses and two public houses (the Old Bear and the Britannia) in Church Street were demolished to allow the construction of the railway tunnel.

Preparations for the digging of the tunnel, Church Street.

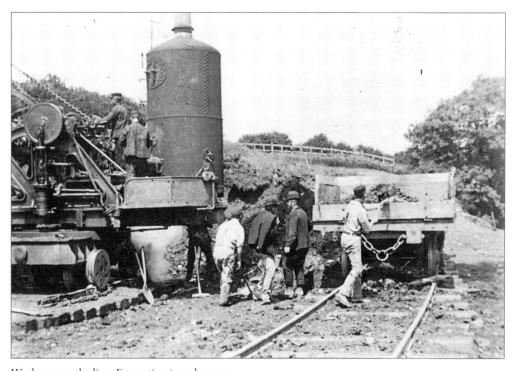

Workmen on the line. Excavation is under way.

The accommodation that was provided at Parsley Hay for the railway workers.

Spen Lane Bridge, taking the railway line over the Ashbourne to Thorpe road.

A railway engine was towed on a wagon by traction engines up Church Street, St John Street, through the market-place, to Dove House Green and down to the end of the tunnel on Mappleton Road. It took three traction engines because of the gradients.

The third traction engine, on its way to lend assistance, goes past the Red Lion and turns into the market-place.

The engine on the new line.

The first engine on the line at Mappleton. It appears to be rolling backwards down the gradient.

A traction engine at Mappleton. The line is continuing to Thorpe and Parsley Hay. Tan Yard Farm is on the left.

Seven Arches Viaduct, c. 1929. It was demolished in the 1960s. The dog in the foreground is named Pepper!

The railway was opened on 1 August 1899. This photograph shows the 2nd VB Notts and Derby Regiment 'C' Company at the opening ceremony.

The station, opening ceremony.

Perhaps this was the first train to run on the line. The driver may have been Mr Ridley, while the guard was Mr Goodall.

The first railway station, later the goods station, and staff, Clifton Road.

The footbridge from the station to Clifton Road.

A sad occasion: the last train to leave in 1964. Ashbourne station was closed as part of the Beeching cutbacks. Fred Hambleton is in the cab. Also present are Roger Wright, Mr Grimshaw, Dr Hollick, Dennis Moore, D. Fletcher, Alec Jones, Arthur Parry, Fred Spencer, Peter Thornly, Roger Winstone, W. Foster, George Rose, Tim Rose, Mr Wigley, Albert Dawson, Fred Birch and Jesse Brumby.

# DO

This is where Aunt Hannah Ward and her mother, my great Aunt Alice ran their ice cream and lemonade stall — by the gate on the left

*The entrance to Dovedale from the Izaak Walton Hotel, about 4 miles from Ashbourne.*

Hanging Bridge, Mayfield, where sheep stealers once met their end. This bridges the River Dove and is on the border between Derbyshire and Staffordshire. The five pointed arches probably date from the fourteenth century, but they were almost all concealed when the bridge was widened in 1937.

The aftermath of a lorry crash, Hanging Bridge. The lorry belonged to Messrs Gibson and Garlic of Swinton, Manchester, and was laden with accumulators destined for the Rolls-Royce factory in Derby.

Royal Oak Hotel, Hanging Bridge, 1920s. There is a CTC roundel on the wall, and RAC and AA signs hanging on the right.

The approach to Dovedale from the Izaak Walton Hotel.

The Izaak Walton Inn, Dovedale. The name of this hotel commemorates the famous author of *The Compleat Angler*, who often fished in Dovedale.

Dovedale is renowned for its surrounding hills, Thorpe Hill and the mass of Bunster, and the River Dove and its stepping stones, which are sometimes flooded in wet weather.

Ilam Rock is named after the village. It is a limestone pinnacle 1½ miles up Dovedale from the stepping stones, and a favourite attraction for rock climbers.

Ilam Hall is a castellated structure in the Elizabethan style. Holy Cross Church in front of the Hall houses the Russell family monument: Pike Watts Russell is sculpted on his deathbed with his family surrounding him. The tomb of St Bertram is also in the church. Many of Ilam's cottages are built in the Swiss style, and replace earlier houses.

A sale at White's Farm, Castern Hall, near Ilam.

Reynard's Cave. This large arch, 40 ft high and 60 ft wide, is supposedly named after a robber who lived nearby. The ascent to this point was steep, and one used to be able to hire a rope for a few pence.

Tissington Spires, on the Staffordshire side of the Dove, is quite impressive.

The stepping stones across the River Dove. Mr Warren used to bring donkeys here from Ashbourne, so that children could ride across the river, and also up to the Peveril Hotel.

The stepping stones, with donkeys, at the foot of Thorpe Cloud, which is an impressive 942 ft high and has superb views along the dale.

The Straits. Dr Johnson is supposed to have said: 'He who has seen Dovedale has no need to visit the Highlands.'

Two views of Lion Face Rock.

Dovedale under Sharplow.

The bowling party at the Fishing Lodge, which was a resting place in Beresford Dale for the famous fishermen Izaak Walton and Charles Cotton.

# AROUND & ABOUT

*St Mary's Church, Mappleton, sometimes called Little St Paul's. The eighteenth-century building has a short tower crowned with a dome and an octagonal cupola. To the west of the church there are clergymen's widows' almshouses, which date from 1727.*

The New Inn, Alsop-en-le-Dale, on the Buxton Road, *c.* 1900. The stage coach proprietor was Mr Carl
Prince.

St Edmund's Church, Fenny Bentley. Some parts date from 1300, while the Parclose screen, with its flamboyant tracery, dates back to 1519. The tower was renewed in 1850. The Beresford family monument is an alabaster tomb, on which husband and wife lie both tied up in shrouds: no part of them can be seen. Round the edge of the tomb there are helmets, shields, breastplates, swords, banners and drums. On one side are depicted the five Beresford daughters; on the other side their sixteen sons – all wearing shrouds.

The interior of St Edward's Church, Fenny Bentley.

Fenny Bentley Hall is now a farm. The square medieval tower is reminiscent of pele towers in the north of England.

Woodeaves, near Fenny Bentley. Mr Nuttall had a cheese factory here. T.J. Potter retired here before moving to Matlock.

An entrance to the Okeover estate, owned by the Walker Okeover family. The Okeover family is one of the oldest in the area, having been here for over eight hundred years, until 1955 in direct male succession. Members of the family have filled offices of honour and trust in the county and elsewhere.

Okeover Hall is a red brick Elizabethan or Jacobean house, rebuilt in 1745 to a design by Joseph Sanderson, and stands elegantly next to the small church, which is being restored. The Hall is still a family residence.

Osmaston Manor was a large neo-Tudor mansion, built by Stevens in 1846–9. It was another home for the Walker Okeovers, but was demolished in 1966. There were extensive Italianate terraces with a palm house, loggia and a 150 ft tower (which still survives); in the park there was a polo ground. In the village there are several thatched cottages. Ashbourne Show is held annually at Osmaston.

The elk pound, Osmaston Manor.

Thomas Moore (1779–1852), poet, lived at this cottage in Mayfield for a short time. He was famous for his poem inspired by the bells of St Oswald's: 'Those evening bells! those evening bells! How many a tale their music tells, Of youth and home, and that sweet time When last I heard their soothing chime.'

Lode Mill and the pack horse bridge, near Alstonefield.

St Peter's Church, Alstonefield. There are some fine carved oak box pews, and Charles Cotton's pew.

Callow Hall on the Mappleton road. This house was built in 1852 by H.I. Stevens of Derby for Mr Goodwin Johnson. It used to be owned by the Longdons but is now a hotel owned by David Spencer and family.

The Green Hall at Offcote, a mile away from Ashbourne, is supposed to have Tudor origins – and inside there is timber framing.

Throwley Hall, near Ilam, was the seat of the Meverells until the seventeenth century, when Lord Cromwell, Earl of Ardglass in Ireland, inherited the estate from his mother, heiress of Robert Meverell. Robert is buried in Ilam church. The Hall has just been restored.

The Peveril Hotel is in Thorpe, near one of the entrances to Dovedale.

Tissington Hall, home of the Fitzherberts – an old county family. The present occupier is Sir Richard Fitzherbert. The Hall is mainly Jacobean, but the library wing dates from 1906.

Tissington Wells Dressing, 1890s. There are five wells, one of which is dressed by schoolchildren. The photograph shows the Hall Well (opposite the Hall), and the others are named the Town, Coffin, Hands and Yew Tree wells. They attract many visitors on Ascension Day and are on show for a week, weather permitting. The well dressing tradition, according to one tradition, began in 1350. During the Black Death (1348–9) many people died because of contaminated water supplies. At Tissington, though, the wells stayed pure and no-one died. To give thanks for this the wells were decorated every year. Another tradition records that the well dressing ceremony dates fron 1615, when Tissington's wells didn't fail during a drought. The custom died out, but was revived in 1950.

All Saints' Church, Bradley. The nave and chancel were rebuilt in the fourteenth century. There are many interesting carvings inside, and also a thirteenth-century font.

Stydd Hall, 1 mile west of Yeaveley. This fine Tudor red-brick house, built on medieval foundations, is now a farmhouse.

The Durham Inn, Compton. James Porter was the landlord when this photograph was taken, during the jubilee celebrations in 1897.

Clifton. Holy Trinity Church, just visible in the background, was built in 1845. Clifton Hall railings are on the right.

The old toll gate on the Ashbourne road into Clifton. The toll house is still there today.

Clifton School, 1926. The picture includes the following: back row: Albert Gerard, Charles Stevenson, Arthur Wilson, Wilfred Gerrard; second row: Bill Rowe, Billy Thacker, Albert Bowler, Bill Melbourne, Sam Ford, Alec Robinson, Chitty Hunter; third row: Dorothy Coxon, Tootsy Burtonshaw, Linda Harrison, May Stone, Dorothy Prince, Miss Glover (teacher); front row: Jack Wilson, Betty Bott, Nancy Key, Stan Robinson, Molly Bott.

Clifton railway station. The stationmaster, Mr Goodall, is leaning on the fence. This was on the North Staffordshire line to Ashbourne and Buxton.

The lodge at Simpson's Mill, Mayfield. The private railway line to the mill from Clifton station is in the foreground.

A goods train, pulled by British Railways tank engine 42605 passes through Clifton station and across the level crossing.

A Nestlé's milk lorry crashed into a train at Clifton station, having passed through the (closed) level crossing gates. Mr Melbourne, the driver, was killed instantly.

Clifton post office: the postmistress, postman and delivery boy.

# ACKNOWLEDGEMENTS

I would like to thank all my friends and relations who have helped me to compile this book, and everyone who has lent me photographs. This book would not have been possible without them.

I would also like to take this opportunity to remember my grandfather, who died in 1923. Many of his photographs, of Ashbourne itself and of the building of the railway, are included here.

# BRITAIN IN OLD PHOTOGRAPHS

To order any of these titles please telephone our distributor, Littlehampton Book Services on 01903 721596
For a catalogue of these and our other titles please ring Regina Schinner on 01453 731114